HAROLD PINTER
A Celebration

HAROLD PINTER

A Celebration

Introduced by
RICHARD EYRE

faber and faber

First published in 2000
by Faber and Faber Limited
3 Queen Square London WC1N 3AU

Typeset by Country Setting, Kingsdown, Kent CT14 8ES
Printed in England by Clays Ltd, St Ives plc

A CIP record for this book
is available from the British Library

0-571-20661-1

2 4 6 8 10 9 7 5 3 1

CONTENTS

———————————

Richard Eyre

Harold Pinter at Seventy

Philip Larkin feared that he'd be memorialised by thousands of schoolchildren in the Albert Hall intoning 'They fuck you up, your Mum and Dad'. It's possible Harold Pinter's nightmare is of the same children chanting 'I have to get to Sidcup for my papers', in which case he will be relieved that his seventieth birthday is being celebrated by friends, collaborators and admirers in this collection of essays. Like Larkin, Pinter has become adjectival, his work has entered the cultural bloodstream: he's become part of who and what we are.

What I am, is a child of the 1950s who grew up in West Dorset knowing as much about theatre as I did about the insect life of Samoa. There were no theatres, at least ones which presented plays, so by the age of eighteen I had seen only two professional productions: Peter O'Toole – pre-Lawrence of Arabia with dark hair and a boxer's nose – as a brilliant Hamlet at the Bristol Old Vic, and Christopher Plummer as a mercurial Benedick at Stratford. And then I saw *The Caretaker*. I hadn't been corrupted by reading about the 'Theatre of the Absurd' or by the critics' passion for kennelling a writer in a category, and I was innocent of the writer's supposed concerns with 'status' and 'territory'. The play seemed to me a natural way of looking at the world, unpredictable but as inevitable as the weather.

I loved the way that the play didn't glut you with exposition, things just happened in it and their significance wasn't spelled out. What it was about seemed irrelevant, what was important was what it was: a world like ours where the meaning of things was at best opaque and the most normal condition of life was uncertainty.

Above all it distilled normal speech – the kind you'd hear on a bus or in a café – into a singular language syncopated with hard wit and percussive poetry. And it used silence as a dramatic tool. It woke me up to the fact that theatre was as much about the spaces between the words as the words themselves, that what was left off the stage was as important as what was put on it, and that feelings – particularly of men – are articulated obliquely or mutely, mostly remaining trapped like water under an icecap.

The 'voice' of the play was recognisable and yet alien, like a familiar object viewed from an unusual angle. The author of *The Caretaker* had a way of looking at the world that was as original as Francis Bacon, whom I once saw standing at a bus stop, the strong wind pasting back his hair and flattening his face: he looked like a Francis Bacon. It's not unusual to have that experience with Harold. I overheard this exchange with a friend of his:

FRIEND: How are you feeling, Harold?
HAROLD: What sort of question is that?

Which is the sort of question asked by a man who is sometimes pugnacious and occasionally splenetic, but is just as often droll and generous – particularly to actors, directors and (a rare quality this) other writers. Sometimes grandiose and occasionally intolerant (which once prompted his friend Simon Gray to say that his heart is with the tyrants which is why he writes them so well), he can be disarmingly modest, unostentatious and comradely. And he is never, ever, afraid to speak his mind, particularly on political matters.

It shouldn't therefore be a surprise that the most powerful piece of political theatre I have ever seen was in Prague at the Cinoherni Theatre in 1969 shortly after the Russian invasion – a play about totalitarianism, persecution, freedom, fear and kindness, called *The Birthday Party*. At the start of rehearsals for the first production of the play, Harold was persuaded by the director, Peter Wood, to say something to the actors about its meaning. 'Just put it on the table that Goldberg and McCann are the socio-politico-religious monsters with whom we are faced, and the pressures on any given individual.' He saw it, as he said: 'very, very, strongly and very, very, clearly at the time. I knew it was political, but I wouldn't just stand on a soap box and say so.'

By the age of fifteen Harold had become passionately engaged by the Labour victory of 1945, which is a powerful ingredient in his considerable contempt for the way New Labour regards the Old Labour Party. He never had the luxury of choice about being political: growing up in a Jewish community during the war, aware of how close he could have been to the fate of many of his relatives, made him aware of the precariousness of democracy and the need to safeguard it. The Bomb and the Cold War turned him into a conscientious objector against National Service, a courageous position which led to two tribunals, two trials and the threat of prison. 'I took my toothbrush along to the trial,' said Harold, 'and it was my first, if you like, overt political act.'

If he didn't go to prison for his beliefs, he might well have done for the theft of a copy of Beckett's *Murphy* from Bermondsey Public Reserve Library (a tributary of the Westminster Library) in 1952, the crime amply justified by the fact that it had last been borrowed in 1939. This dogged persistence to hunt down the work of a writer whom he had previously only encountered in an Irish literary magazine would seem to support the biblical genealogy of theatre history: Samuel Beckett begat Harold Pinter. But the truth is that Harold's work, while having things in common with Beckett and Joyce (and Kafka for that matter), is entirely *sui generis*: he has always spoken with his own voice and I hope that nothing will diminish its power to move and enchant in the theatre, to provoke and ignite outside it, and to go on exhorting us that art and politics matter.

All the contributions in this book testify to Harold being, as he said of Arthur Miller, 'a hell of a fellow': a cricketer, a defender of human rights, a passionate polemicist, a playwright of rare power and profound originality, a lucid director and an actor who always surprises and never disappoints.

Happy birthday, Harold.

HAROLD PINTER
A Celebration

EDNA O'BRIEN

Memo

Nights of wine and reminiscence
Anew McMaster extolling in Athlone
Black pudding breakfasts with Pat Magee
Bristling over a missing jock strap.
That time in old Yugoslavia –
The pavements satiny underfoot,
And your recurring love of Webster,
The way you run your hands over your eyes
And search maddeningly for your glasses
As for the defining word.
When you dream
Do you dream of those rooms
That were your first abode,
Brown rooms lit with language,
A tacit pair
Keeping the hours
Talking of this and that
And the malevolent tread.
Midnight's fat shadow
The quiet sweat.
To know you is merely to guess
At your battered rooms.

Beannact leat.

ALAN BATES

_____

My agent told me that I'd been offered a play at the Arts Theatre which he couldn't make head nor tail of and the pay was £6 per week. He said I'd had a better offer from BBC Television: 'So there's nothing to discuss, is there?' I said I didn't understand the play either but that I'd had an instinctive reaction to its poetry and humanity and I would definitely be doing it. My agent attended the first night and was first round at my dressing room door. To his great credit he said, 'Never listen to me again.' The play was, of course, *The Caretaker*.

Harold's work as a writer has been acclaimed over and over again, quite rightly, but it is about his work as a director that I feel I can say something. He is the sort of director that one dreams about: his objectivity, his courtesy to everyone working with him, and his absolute clarity in his interpretation of other people's writing. I worked with him on plays by Simon Gray and Harold's delight in Simon's comedy, eloquence and great understanding of human behaviour was terrific.

Harold as a director inspires confidence and has an appreciation of what everyone else has to offer. With him it is a truly shared experience.

RONALD HARWOOD

Perhaps we should have played a tie-break. Harold and I against Antonia Fraser's son, Orlando, a barrister, and his friend, Xandy Beckett, a painter. Their combined ages totalled fifty years; Harold's and mine, one hundred and twenty-five. They won 19–17 but only after we had run them ragged, and were ourselves exhausted.

The match was played in the late afternoon at the Vanderbilt Racquet Club in Shepherd's Bush. It lasted two hours, possibly longer. God knows how I managed to drive back home to Chelsea. I remember heaving myself out of the car and being too weary to climb the stairs to my bedroom, so I flopped down in front of the television, glassy-eyed and flushed with defeat, to watch something mindless. Harold telephoned. We relived our pleasure. He, too, was feeling weary – not something he usually likes to admit. I have never found out how the juniors fared. They probably went off to a seedy club and danced till dawn. It was one of the best men's doubles I have ever played, certainly the longest, and Harold and I still talk of it, often.

Harold came to lawn tennis late and, apart from a weak first service, took naturally to the game, developing into a good doubles player. He is especially dazzling at the net. Little gets by him and he's difficult to lob because he has what ballet dancers call elevation, and because of his speed around the court, which is astonishing. Age doesn't seem to have slowed him down. To play tennis with Harold, or any game for that matter, is to enter into a gladiatorial arena, where every point is taken with deadly seriousness as though you're in a final at Wimbledon. A friendly contest is transformed into high drama. He calls a fault loudly but sometimes too quickly and triumphantly. No idle chatter as he passes you when you're changing ends. As a matter of fact, he avoids looking at you as though he wants to make quite sure that you won't misinterpret a fleeting glance as a sign of weakness. Occasionally, during a game, he'll make a withering comment. I recall playing a mixed doubles against him and Antonia, and using the drop-shot to good effect. 'Are you going to do that all the time?' he asked, glowering. 'No, not all the time,' I said rather lamely, but continued to play it as often as possible. The point is you have to keep your nerve if you're not to be intimidated.

But more often than not, in our mixed doubles matches, Antonia and I played as partners. She is steady as a rock at the back of the court and her lobs would make Steffi Graf envious. We had two recurring comments. If we lost, we'd say with superior smiles, 'But then, we're artists.' If Harold played a particularly devilish shot, we'd describe it as 'unchristian'.

I first clapped eyes on Harold on 7 December 1952 but that's not why I remember the date so precisely. I remember it for two other reasons: first, because it was a year to the day that I had left South Africa and, second, because it happened to be the day I was employed by Donald Wolfit. He was seeing actors at the Waldorf Hotel in Aldwych. London was shrouded in a Sherlock Holmes fog, one of the last of the great pea-soupers, ominous, eerie, auspicious. And it was while waiting in the lobby for my interview that I saw a dark and handsome young man come bounding down the stairs to embrace a gorgeous red-headed girl, and exclaim, 'I've got it! I've got it!' (Years later, I learned from John Osborne that he, too, was interviewed for a job that afternoon but wasn't as fortunate.)

The Donald Wolfit Shakespeare Company opened its season in February of the following year at the King's Theatre, Hammersmith, with *Oedipus the King* and *Oedipus at Colonus* played on the same night. Harold was in the chorus; Sir Lewis Casson was the blind Teiresias and I led him on in the first play, and was a guard in a heavy, uncomfortable fireman's helmet in the second. Harold and I did not become friends then. He was senior and I suspect rather disapproved of me. I was, probably still am, rather too ebullient and given to showing off. He was apt to take the piss, which is, by the way, another of his great sporting talents. For the uninitiated, taking the piss is a form of teasing, but teasing is altogether too effete a word. Taking the piss, when performed by a master, is usually a somewhat steely pursuit, intended to discomfort and unsettle. Harold is, without doubt, one of the best piss-takers on the planet. The difficulty is knowing when he's doing it.

We saw each other rarely after the Wolfit season and did not become real friends until the late Penelope Mortimer invited us to a dinner party in 1968. During the course of the evening, we discovered that we had both recently taken up squash and that we were members of the MCC which meant we could play at Lord's. A match was arranged for the following week; it was to be the first of many, and it was also the beginning of a friendship that has meant much to me and, I hope, to Harold. He has been loyal and supportive. We have never had a row. (I once pointed this out to him. 'Well, *you* must be fucking remarkable,' he said.) We have worked together professionally only once since our Wolfit days when he directed my play *Taking Sides*. He is the best of directors but, more importantly, the best of friends.

Those years when we played squash regularly at Lord's were lovely times. Although we were both heavy smokers – I still am but Harold has long since given up his black Balkan Sobranies – we played hard, fierce matches. I am not sure how good we were but, my God, we certainly gave it everything we had.

Lord's did the squash and Real Tennis players proud. There was an elderly attendant named George who ran our baths in private changing rooms and laid out our clothes. The bath-tubs were side by side but separated by a thin wooden partition. As we soaked in water heated to a perfect temperature, I could hear him coughing his lungs out and, without doubt, he could hear me. Afterwards, we'd have a drink at the bar at the back of the Real Tennis court and it was there, in the mid-seventies, that he told me he'd fallen in love with Antonia. Thirst partially quenched, we'd set off for a restaurant and undo all the good we were supposed to have gained from the squash.

I had met Antonia but did not really know her until she and Harold came together. In the fraught times when the media were pursuing them, they used to come down for weekends to Liss in Hampshire where we then lived. My wife, Natasha, who is a glorious cook, provided sumptuous meals. And the four of us would talk and talk into the early hours, champagne flowing. I remember once making scrambled eggs on toast at about three in the morning. Harold, I think, was impressed.

Cricket, of course, is one of the great passions of Harold's life, as it is of mine. But he is truly knowledgeable and has a wonderful memory for the games he has seen or read about, for the players, past and present, and for the literature of cricket. We have watched test matches and county matches together but it doesn't do to introduce into conversation, say, the latest theatre gossip. You are there to watch and concentrate on the cricket and for no other reason. No one I know is able to live in the moment, any moment, in the way Harold does.

I played several times for the Harold Pinter xi, not to be confused with his beloved Gaieties side of which he was the captain and later *eminence blanc*. The Harold Pinter xi was a scratch team – the players included, among others, Simon Gray, Tom Courtenay and Tom Stoppard, who kept wicket – and we played mostly against an eleven from the *Guardian* newspaper. Once, John Hurt, the actor and a useful fast bowler, arrived late, just as we were about to take the field. While he was hurriedly changing Harold looked at him disapprovingly. Hurt was aware of the unspoken reproach and said, 'I know you're famous for the economy of your language, Harold, but your directions for getting here were fucking ridiculous.' Harold sort of smiled.

If I have made my point that Harold takes tennis and squash seriously, then when it comes to cricket it is necessary to enter another dimension. For example, at our level, it is the custom to applaud the opposing captain when he comes in to bat. We dutifully did this – but only once. Harold snapped, 'Cut that out, it's totally meaningless.' He is said to have dropped Tom Courtenay from the side because Tom, a dour Yorkshire opening bat, scored too slowly. And to leave the ground, for whatever reason, before the final ball is bowled is considered the most serious crime in the calendar: it produces in Harold disappointment and anger, mostly the latter.

Sir Leonard Hutton was his hero, which tells you much. Hutton, one of the most illustrious cricketers of the twentieth century, batted with the kind of intensity and economy that is evident in every aspect of Harold's work and life. And Hutton scored a great many runs. So, in one way or another, has Harold.

EILEEN DISS

During the fifties and sixties I was a designer at the BBC and knew, as we all did, Harold Pinter's plays for theatre and television, but I didn't actually work on one until 1965, when the BBC mounted *The Tea Party* for the European Broadcasting Union, an ambitious project in which the play was transmitted in the same week by other European countries in their several languages.

The Basement followed, in which Harold himself took the part of Stott, but the first time I worked with him as a director was for his memorable production of James Joyce's *Exiles* at Bernard Miles' Mermaid Theatre in 1970. It was an exciting but unnerving experience. There was very little money and the set was built on the premises by a very individual carpenter known as 'Smudge'. I was appalled to find that by the morning of the technical rehearsal on stage we had only the basic element with just bare openings for doors and windows, and absolutely nil in the way of atmosphere.

Harold took it in his stride, and by the time we opened it was more or less in place and certainly didn't detract from the beautifully acted and directed performances, but it wasn't a good beginning.

I thought this might be the first and last time I would have the pleasure of designing a set for Harold, but in fact over the thirty years that have gone by since then there have been many occasions, all of them enjoyable and illuminating.

Harold's approach has always been straightforward and direct; no flights of fancy or self-indulgent interpretations that have little to do with the understanding of the text, which is always paramount in his productions.

His rehearsals are very disciplined: no late arrivals, no noise from outside, no interruptions. He creates an atmosphere of concentration which is not as severe as it might sound, and is certainly appreciated by the cast. Afterwards it's a different story; Harold is a gregarious soul and a generous and hospitable one. It's a great pleasure to be in his company, especially as he does seem to have a genuine affection for women, not always found in directors.

He also has an almost pathological dislike of extraneous noise, whether it's unwelcome music in a wine bar or (much worse) something happening in or outside the rehearsal room or theatre.

I remember giving five pounds to a loud guitar player outside the flimsy walls of Hampstead Theatre to 'please go away' during the technical rehearsal of *The Hothouse*, and am deeply ashamed that my own horrible mobile phone rang during the last hushed moments of the read-through of *Ashes to Ashes*. It was a ghastly moment. Every head turned towards me in horror; it must have looked just like one of those Bateman cartoons in *Punch*.

Harold was remarkably nice about it; I expected a thunderbolt but he merely said, 'I don't suppose you'll ever do that again,' and indeed I've been neurotic about the damned thing ever since.

Although I can't claim to have been close to Harold other than professionally, I do feel a strong empathy with his background, coming from the same kind of upright and loving East London parents without much money, being an only child and having a very secure childhood interrupted by war and evacuation and later on attending the local grammar school and going to the People's Palace in Mile End on Sunday evenings to see foreign films.

Like many people, I used to think of Harold as non-political until I heard about his conscientious objection to National Service and began to realise his involvement in a dozen different struggles against injustice throughout the world. What is so impressive about his commitment is that he could so easily confine himself comfortably to his success in the world of literature and drama, but has this passion for truth and justice without seeming to care at all about the hostility it frequently earns him.

I admire him for his humanity, humour, lack of intellectual or any other kind of snobbery, loyalty to friends and colleagues, straightforwardness and above all his integrity.

Whereas most of us of Harold's generation are getting a bit tired these days one way or another, Harold isn't; he epitomises more than anyone I have ever known Shaw's 'life force'.

Long may he continue to do so.

DAVID HARE

———————

I first heard of Harold Pinter when I was at school. I think I'd read a play of his when I was about thirteen, but it never occurred to me he actually existed. Later, our Modern Languages master, Harry Guest, went up to London for the weekend and attended an intense, smoky party in what for me was still the mythical capital city, and found himself in deep conversation with the most admired young playwright of the day. Harry told us about it during our French lesson soon after. To all of us schoolboys, stuck away in the freezing cold of Sussex in the early 1960s, it seemed an impossibly glamorous encounter. You may imagine my astonishment when I found that this same Harold Pinter, who seemed so alluringly continental, actually lived just five miles away, in the unlikely seaside town of Worthing.

I wrote to him, of course, drawing his attention to this remarkable coincidence – that, unbeknown to him, he lived so close to a snotty little schoolboy who liked his work. In those days Pinter seemed to spend a good part of his time warding off zealous commentary on his output. Since most of that commentary came wrapped in the head-freezing jargon of the day – 'failure of communication', 'hidden menace' and so on – I think he was wise to keep his distance. I, meanwhile, had been allocated the job of writing an essay for the school literary society. As I remember, it was called

'Osborne and Pinter: Two Types of Realism'. Like most such critical intruders, I received no reply.

Even at that early age, I could see that Pinter was an unusual figure. Now, almost forty years later, it is clear that British culture has been distorted by a false, contemporary division between literature and the performing arts. In France you find Marguerite Duras, Sartre and Camus all regarding the theatre as one of the necessary, even one of the defining places for a person of letters to do their work. In Ireland, you find Beckett and Yeats with the same idea. Perversely, it is only here in what Betjeman called 'dear old, bloody old England', where the tradition of theatre has always been strongest, that a purple vein of snobbery runs through the broadsheet book pages and through the attitudes of some poets and novelists themselves. It is only here, in a country still marked out by its gift for the performing arts, that literary folk seem threatened by the prospect of working in a form founded in the notion of collaboration.

From the very start, Pinter was inspiring because he was an obvious intellectual, and not ashamed to show it. He was a man who had read and absorbed European ideas and who wanted to explode them, with a terrifying bang, into English working-class settings. Up till then, poets who strayed into the English-speaking theatre often seemed pretentious (Lawrence Durrell) or dazzlingly incompetent (T. S. Eliot). But Pinter was a rare example of someone who was able to marry the intensity of his vision to a simple, practical mastery of his form. One of the many things Pinter has done for the culture of his day is to remind the literary world that you don't always find a poet between the covers of a book.

The work of most good writers is born out of contra-diction. Snoo Wilson once wrote perceptively that John Osborne was a perfect Edwardian because he embodied the most notable archetypes of the period: he was both gentleman and cad. Harold Pinter, by contrast, belongs firmly to the mid-twentieth century, because in him you find expressed the great struggle of the period – between primitive rage on the one hand and liberal generosity on the other. Anyone who meets Harold quickly becomes charmed by his volatility, which has always seemed to me only a by-product of his openness. Because Harold does actually listen to what you say, there is a better-than-even chance that he will also react to it. This surprises some people. As an artist, Pinter has an alarming range. He can play great, big major chords made up only of anger, indignation and contempt. But, at the other end of the instrument, Pinter can also unbalance you by reaching humour, grace and intense personal warmth.

Attending a recent revival of *The Homecoming*, directed by Roger Michell, I was reminded not just of how bold Pinter himself used to be, but how uncompromising the whole theatre was forty years ago in its willingness to shock and disturb its audience. Even after so many years, the play still took the audience aback, not in any obvious four-letter way, but because it was so naked, so shameless in its portrayal of a knock-down sexual struggle within a family. Never for a moment was the audience allowed the get-out of doubting that something real and important was at stake. Much is always made of Pinter's style. But it's his many imitators who now copy the style and don't notice the content. The impact of this exceptional evening depended on Pinter keeping his guard high, so that he never once offered the spectator the easy handhold of an 'attitude' with which they might be able to take some simplified view of the events on the stage.

It's this uncompromising approach to an audience, this willingness to say 'take it or leave it' (again, in my view, both generous and brutal) which is, I believe, Pinter's most distinctive and lasting contribution to the theatre. It does not surprise me at all that the author himself was thrilled when, after a performance of *Ashes to Ashes* in New York, a member of the audience was heard to remark, 'And he has the brass balls to call this a play?' Rarely can a playwright have combined so much nerve, so much gall with so much evident pleasure in that gall.

Beyond that, it's the familiar mark of a first-rate artist that we all have our own favoured part of his or her work. Ibsenites dispute over whether to prefer the verse plays or the social plays. Fans of John Ford argue fiercely about whether his Westerns go up- or down-hill as he gets older. Pinter sometimes seems as various as his admirers, but my own playwright is the one who gives you the three-course luncheon, the same man who wrote a trio of formidable, full-length plays in quick succession – *The Birthday Party*, *The Caretaker* and *The Homecoming* – while managing with his spare hand to develop two of the most perfect screenplays ever offered to the British cinema, for Joseph Losey's films of *The Servant* and *Accident*. Something majestic happens when a minimalist decides to go the whole distance.

The interpretation of living writers' work is an approximate business at best, and, in Pinter's case, you never seem to find the critical tea-trolley in the same place twice. I don't find current protestations that Harold was always a political playwright any more convincing than the things which were written when people lumped him, even more crudely, into the Theatre of the Absurd. It's quite clear that Harold – like Patrick White, whom he resembles – went through a period of antagonism to politics, both in theatre and in life, which was as profound, in its way, as his more recent, exemplary advocacy of some very important causes. A lot of people like to claim that, without Beckett, Pinter couldn't have existed.

Again, I can't say I really know what this means. With his own highly original temperament and technique, it seems hard to believe that Pinter wouldn't have burst out at us in one way or another.

If, on the occasion of his seventieth birthday, we want to agree on anything, then we can agree on this: Pinter did what Auden said a poet should do. He cleaned the gutters of the English language, so that it ever afterwards flowed more easily and more cleanly. We can also say that over his work and over his person hovers a sort of leonine, predatory spirit which is all the more powerful for being held under in a rigid discipline of form, or in a black suit. Almost alone among British playwrights he has excelled as much when adapting others and when writing for the screen as he has when writing for the stage. The essence of his singular appeal is that you sit down to every play or film he writes in certain expectation of the unexpected. In sum, this tribute from one writer to another: you never know what the hell's coming next.

DOUGLAS HODGE

———————————

I don't know what you'd ever give a bloke like that for a birthday present. Maybe the clink of a pebble as it passes to the pocket, the sound of sheer stockings under a dress, a cross-court volley from a backhand topspin – just in, a Larkin quote, a kick up the old Dictator's arse, the clash of ice cubes in a whisky glass, two men in an empty room, a proscenium arch, no salad, no fizzy water and an actor– manager. I'd shut down the air conditioning and stop them screaming outside, a long leg, a conscientious objector, a cover drive off a googly. No fucking coughing and words like nary, amanuensis, stair-rod, Double Diamond, physiotherapist and names from the Cenotaph and an almanac. A dab hand at ping pong, a first run-through, an arm wrestle, a preview – an opening night meal, Buñuel, *The Dead*, the sanity clause, a bomb under the U. S. of A. brother, Alfred Brendel, the love of a mother, The Ivy, The Caprice, the silence when an audience breathes as one. The fifty-yard sprint, A. F., the first round the block, a Russian Sobranie Black, Noël Coward, a kiss in the back of a cab, bludbrudershaft, a suede jacket and shoes, Flamineo's steel, *Le Chien Andalou*, Goldberg and Sacks and 'Raitch. The love of a Dad, the love of a son, Mauritius, jacaranda, hibiscus and bougainvillea, the World Bank's bollox, the memory of Proust, Auntie Mary's canary and Kafka's closed door. I'd tickle his arse with a feather, whip off his glasses, silence the traffic and chill the white wine in the fridge. At Clapton Pond, at silly mid-on, Sidcup and Arthur Miller. Six thousand buckets, the aristocracy, Cornwall during the war, the Marx Brothers and *King Lear*. The freedom to breathe and write and not write. My own complete friendship, loyalty and thanks. Manners, civility, celerity, precision, class and clarity. What man could ask for more?

PENELOPE WILTON

I first met Harold twenty-three years ago when I went to audition for his new play *Betrayal*, which Peter Hall was directing at the National Theatre.

Leaving my six-month-old baby in the casting director's office, I was taken down to a rehearsal room and introduced to Harold and Peter. I can't remember a lot being said about the play or the part. I read a scene or two; they said 'thank you' and I left feeling rather flushed, nervous and relieved. I climbed the stairs to retrieve from whoever it was that was holding a now screaming child, thanking them and as usual apologising for the inconvenience I must have caused. Suddenly Harold appeared in the doorway. 'Penelope, I would like you to be my Emma.' It was like being given the most wonderful present.

So started a professional relationship that has meant the world to me.

The rehearsal began in one of those ghastly cavernous rehearsal rooms that are fine when filled with people, but feel so lonely when there are only three actors and two dark-suited men gazing at you like God and the Holy Ghost.

Michael Gambon, Daniel Massey (my then husband) and myself worked well together, although we had our ups and downs – it wasn't easy. Harold didn't say a great deal.

One morning Michael and I were rehearsing a scene where he had to take me in his arms, embrace and kiss me. We didn't seem to be getting it right, and after a while Harold got up and came over to where we were standing and said to Michael, 'Do you mind if I show you how?' He then turned to Dan who was watching and said, 'Do you mind if I hold your wife?'

Harold, I don't think, ever presumes anything.

So we came to the opening previews, a nerve-wracking time, waiting in the dark on stage, a hushed auditorium . . . a slow fade-up and there we are, sitting at a table in a bar, Michael moving over with two drinks, a glass of white wine for me and a pint of beer for himself. Only because it's the first preview of Harold's play, we are both thinking, 'When I open my mouth, will any sound come out?' Michael puts the pint in front of me and the wine in front of himself. I look down and think, 'Fuck, I've got to drink two of these!' I look up and we smile at each other, and as we reach for the drinks he realizes what he's done and switches the glasses – relief! We toast each other, but a little too quickly; the glass hits his teeth and sends a spray of beer all over his face. Of course we get over it, and much much later we laugh, but oh . . .

I have had the pleasure, the excitement, the *thrill* of seeing all of Harold's plays, watching him act and being directed by him. To have had such a companion to walk with through a career is the thing that dreams are made of.

PATRICK MARBER

_____

When I was fourteen I went to New York with my parents.

Through a family friend I met the celebrated drama critic, Jack Kroll. We were in his office at *Newsweek* when he asked me what I wanted to do with my life. I said I thought I might like to write plays, if I could.

'Would you now?' He handed me a Grove Press edition of *Pinter: Plays One* and said, 'You'd better have this then.'

In 1980, I saw *The Caretaker*. I got a standby ticket and sat in the stalls of the Lyttelton, second row, straight up their noses. The actors were Ken Cranham, Jonathan Pryce and Warren Mitchell.

I was mesmerised. At the end of the evening I walked back to Waterloo Station elated.

The following year, at school, we did a production of *The Caretaker*.

It was an 'unofficial' production, a labour of love, not a school play.

We three 'actors' directed it ourselves, in a classroom, 'in the round'.

We spent a term scavenging for junk and rehearsing whenever we could. We played for three nights. I was 'Davies'. I still see 'Aston' now and then. He's called John Metcalfe. He remembers the long walk up the stairs to make our first entrance. He plays the viola extremely well. In fact, he does it for a living.

At university I acted in a few plays. I was in a production of *Betrayal*.

My twenty-one-year-old 'Robert' was akin to my seventeen-year-old 'Davies': a lethal combination of enthusiasm and incompetence.

I studied English Literature. I wrote about Pinter in my finals: 'Modern Drama'. I don't recall what I wrote but I do remember 'padding out' my arguments with extensive and excessive quotation from two of his plays.

In 1993 I wrote my first play. In 1995 it was put on at the National Theatre. One night, I was knocking around the lighting box just before curtain up.

'Anyone in?'

Fiona Bardsley, the Deputy Stage Manager, said, 'Harold Pinter.'

'Yeah, yeah.'

'No, really.'

I scanned the stalls and found him on the end of a row. I stayed and watched the first ten minutes. Or rather, I watched the back of Pinter's head watching the first ten minutes. The head did not fall off with laughter but nor did it twitch with irritation. Nor did it cough. A few days later I received a little note from him. He said he'd had a whale of a time and that he wished me more power to my elbow. I kept the note in my breast pocket for a month.

A few weeks later I was at a literary party. My first play changed my life: it meant I got invited to literary parties. Harold was there, with Antonia.

I decided to introduce myself and decided to do it pissed.

'Excuse me, sorry, I . . . I . . . I'm . . . my name's Patrick Marber.'

Not a flicker. In fact, agitation perceptible. Realisation now that the note was a fake, probably from a member of the cast.

'I wrote a play called *Dealer's Choice*, I think you might've seen it . . . '

Pause

'Yes! Ah, yes! Antonia, this is the author of *Dealer's Choice*. Bloody good. Come and sit down.'

So I sat down with the Pinters and affected to know a thing or two about cricket.

In May of 1999 I had lunch with Harold. I arrived ten minutes early which is damn early for me. He was there already. He wore a black shirt and drank white wine. In fact, we drank a fair amount of white wine together. I'd put it about, via our mutual agent Judy Daish, that I'd be pretty keen to direct *The Caretaker* and word came back that Harold would not be averse. So we discussed the play in an adult fashion, director to playwright.

I wondered when someone was going to tap me on the shoulder and wake me from this fantasy.

A month or two later I called Harold to discuss some bit of production business. He was in Dorset. He came to the phone, full of beans.

'Hallo, Harold. You sound well.'

'Well I am well. I'm very well. I'm writing a play.'

He spoke like a man who had never written a play before, thrilled and delighted that the words were flowing. I was stabbing around in the dark with a new one. Harold asked after it delicately; he treated me like a fellow writer, as if all writers are equals, all prone to the same problems.

A few weeks later *Celebration* arrived in the post. The bravura energy of the play, its bilious hilarity, seemed like something written by a man half his age. I *am* half his age and the words emerge from *me* like slugs.

Last summer I was directing my second play, *Closer*, on Broadway.

Jack Kroll came to interview me for *Newsweek* magazine. We chatted away in the lobby of the Algonquin where I was staying.

I told him he'd given me a book some twenty years ago and that it had been more than useful. He was delighted. He spoke at some length and with great admiration for and about Harold's work.

Jack Kroll died this summer. It was an honour to have met him.

The book he had given me was upstairs in my hotel room. Why would I ever part with it?

It's here on my desk, as I write.

Happy birthday, Harold. More power to your elbow.

JANET WHITAKER

'Harold Pinter is coming to the readthrough.' Panic. *No Man's Land* is not an easy play and I wasn't sure I understood it all. But with Dirk Bogarde as Spooner and Michael Hordern as Hirst (BBC Radio 3, 1992), it was like an old friends' reunion. I took the plunge and admitted I really didn't understand one part of the play in Act 2 and Harold replied, 'I've never really understood that bit either.' What a lovely man – he'd given me the freedom to get on with my wonderful cast (also including Keith Allen and Bernard Hill) and to make of the play what we could fathom. And it got richer and funnier the deeper we went.

The other best moment – directing Harold as Andy in *Moonlight* (BBC Radio 3, 2000), I suggested that he hold a pause for a bit longer. He gave me a long look, then with a twinkle agreed, as Sara Kestelman (playing Bel) rocked with laughter.

The plays are like dancing through a hall of mirrors, endlessly captivating, full of surprises, reflecting back on themselves, baffling at times and deeply disquieting, but full of such poetry and humour, they are a joy to work on.

Louis Marks

It was sometime in the summer of 1979 that I approached Harold with an invitation to direct a television production of Simon Gray's *The Rear Column* for BBC2's 'Play of the Month' strand. We all met at the National Theatre where they were working together on Simon's latest work, *Close of Play*. *The Rear Column* had closed after a short West End run, directed by Harold, and it seemed to me a good idea to rescue it for a much wider audience, as well as 'immortalising it on tape', as we used to say, which would be a not invaluable side-product. The meeting started a happy professional relationship which lasted many years.

It might not have done. The project was agreed, dates arranged, casting decided and then, the weekend before the start of production, Harold called me to say he'd changed his mind and could not do it. Frantic phone calls ensued. Simon exploded. 'Get another director!' he demanded. I was bewildered, finding myself with an expensive, scheduled production about to go – or rather not go – down the tubes, but also distressed, having set my heart and my hopes on Harold as the key to its success.

I appealed to him to think again. We talked at length and what was clear was that, inexperienced as he was in the technicalities of TV production, he felt simply unable to cope with the task. I did my best to reassure. Anyway, he agreed to think again. He spent the day walking in

Holland Park and called me back that evening to say he was on.

Television drama means filming a performance. Harold was at home directing performances. The problems were essentially about where to place the actors and the cameras. The first rehearsal day arrived. No props. No scenery. Tape stuck on the rehearsal room floor to show the outlines of sets. Notional sticks of furniture. Harold began blocking the action. The first assistant, Mike Jackley (unsung hero of so many BBC TV dramas), interrupted: 'Sorry Harold, but if you place Barry there, camera one will be in camera two's shot.' Harold reconsidered. He rearranged. Eileen Diss, the designer, raised a hand. 'There won't be any scenery behind him there.'

Harold stopped the rehearsal, dismissed all the actors and sat down with Mike and Eileen and began plotting the shots from first principles. It was a steep learning curve but his concentration was total, his grasp of detail extraordinary, his tenacity in pursuing a technical problem impressive. And in an unexpected way, once the principles were grasped, he seemed to be enjoying it hugely. He won the crew's respect. He was in his element.

When we finally got to the recording studio, Harold was positively beaming as he sat at the desk in the control room looking at the banks of monitors. The immediacy of the process, the ability to ask for a second or third take of some speech or piece of action and conjure up the instant result, was a novel and exciting experience. I still believe that there is little to compare with the thrill of capturing moments of great drama when all the elements suddenly come together in the studio, and Harold was clearly exhilarated by it.

So the production went well. Simon was happy too; Harold had mastered a new skill and was eager to have another go. But at what?

In April 1980 *The Hothouse*, which he had written some twenty-two years earlier but put aside for other work, was finally staged and I went to see it at Hampstead with my wife. It seems strange to recall with what awe Pinter was regarded by audiences at that time. Awe is different from respect or admiration. It implies distance; and that night, in that small theatre, the distance between what was happening on stage and how it was registered in the minds of the audience seemed vast. The macabre comedy being played between the pompous Roote and the devious Gibbs concerning the bizarre disappearance of 6457 – or was it 6459? – had my wife and me in stitches. Indeed so loud did we laugh that we were shushed by some of the audience who seemed to think laughter quite out of place, if not blasphemous, at a Pinter play.

I can't remember which of us made the suggestion but it did seem a natural decision to do it for television using the original cast and with Harold this time directing Pinter. It was not a difficult project for me to sell. And this time there were no last-minute nerves. It was a joyous experience and Harold was now much more at home in the medium. His approach was bolder and visually far more inventive. The idea of introducing a hugely imposing staircase into the design which would be seen only occasionally, with no scenes played out on it and only the occasional glimpse of a single character until the end when we saw the shadows of the escaping inmates flitting across, was a brilliant way of conveying the menacing, oppressive inhumanity of the institution.

There was another and, for me, key difference. This was Pinter directing his own text. With *The Rear Column* Simon had always been on hand to talk about meanings, interpretations. With Harold, being Harold, there were no explanations. The lines were the lines. Just say them and they would work. There were no special ways to play the lines to make their meanings clearer or give sub-text to them. Harold had written them, acted them to himself and knew they would communicate themselves to the audience. As for the meaning of the play as a whole, this was never talked about, or even gently broached. Harold's reticence or reluctance to be drawn into any discussions of this nature discouraged questions, or so we took it.

There were many other practical things to talk about concerned with the production. Whatever the issue – schedules, publicity, travel arrangements – Harold was always precise and expected – demanded – precision in return. If he showed impatience, even annoyance, it was when he got imprecise answers. He hated fudge. I came to think of this as one of his greatest strengths, as a man and as a writer.

That sounds severe. Not so. *The Hothouse* was a smooth and very happy production without any major glitches. Harold and I differed seriously on only one point. At the recording I felt the greater naturalism with which he directed the opening scene about the mysteriously dead 6457 (or 6459) detracted from the comic absurdity which in the theatre had kicked the play off with such a burst of energy. It was not a big point but Harold took my doubts seriously and insisted we play it back the next day to see if we would re-shoot it. We did and felt reassured.

So we came to the final stage of the production, the tape editing. The cumbersome editing machines of those days required two editors to work with the director. The key man is a trained and experienced editor. The other is his assistant who plays in the various tapes preparatory to making the cut. The assistant's name was Steve. He was a trainee editor. The process took about three days.

The editing finished, we all felt pleased and repaired to the bar. Harold bought the first round and we toasted the production. Then Steve turned to Harold. 'Tell me Harold, how d'you come to write a play like this?' Silence. We looked into our glasses. 'Well, Steve, I'll tell you,' said Harold. 'Vivien and I were living in Chiswick at the time and we had no money. And I saw this advertisement by the Maudsley Psychiatric Hospital for volunteers to act as guinea-pigs at ten and sixpence a time . . . '. And he went on to tell the story of the room with the electrodes and the shatteringly piercing sound, now widely known and recounted in his biography.

But at that time it was a revelation.

Over the next decade we worked together on television productions of two more of his plays: *One for the Road* (director: Kenneth Ives) and *Mountain Language*, directed by Harold. In 1988 he entrusted me with a proposal for a far more ambitious project: to produce a film of Kafka's *The Trial* which he wanted to write and direct himself. It was the book which more than any other had inspired him to be a writer. The screenplay, which he sent to me in August 1989, was a rich blend of the two seminal writers of the century. But Harold decided against directing it himself. It was eventually filmed in Prague in 1992. The director was David Jones.

As a director, I believe Harold feels his real home is the theatre. But I hope that, looking back, his forays into the television studios at Wood Lane gave him as much fun and gratification as they did me. I look back on them with deep gratitude and affection.

SIMON GRAY

I have known Harold too long to be able to write about him in anything except the immediate, so here's something immediate from the past.

Harold's written a new play, *One for the Road*. It's a crisp and brutal study of an interrogator/torturer going about his business in an unnamed country. (South Africa? Turkey? Albania? Almost anywhere in South Africa today. And probably anywhere else tomorrow.) The chap's name is Nicholas, and we see him having professional chats with three of his victims – a hideously tortured dissident; the dissident's wife who has been subject to all kinds of brutality, including gang rape, to which she will be further subjected; and their eight-year-old son whom Nicholas finally has put to death, a fact he slips to the father in the last line or two of the play. Its running time is about half an hour, I'd guess, which is pretty short in terms of time, but quite long enough in terms of subject. What I like best about it is the ghastly richness of Harold's monster, the seemingly unmotivated switches of mood between bantering playfulness to self-righteous rage followed by a joke that he genuinely wants to share with whichever victim is immediately in his presence.*

---

* Exactly like one of my teachers at prep school, now I come to think of it, although unlike Harold's monster he did the torturing as well as the interrogating. An all-rounder, in other words. I still dream of meeting up with him one day, especially if he's become enfeebled by time.

In fact, it's a study in the absolute power of someone who's gone beyond absolute corruption on to complete freedom of spirit. Which is also complete vacancy. Nicholas isn't simply good at his job, but was positively born to it. I suppose in some ways Nicholas is a relation of Max, Davis, Goldberg and McCann. He'd also find congenial company in Dickens' world – Fagin, Dennis the hangman, Bounderby, the murdering Chuzzlewit. But then Harold's always been a very English writer, rather than the enigmatic European intellectual (Beckett, Kafka, etc.) that academics and critics would like to turn him into. Like Dickens, he can make one laugh in panic.

Harold himself, of course, loves laughter in the theatre, especially when it's provoked by one of his own plays. The cathedral reverence with which they're sometimes received (thanks mainly to the industrious spade-work of English departments and literary journals) must be exasperating. I remember being told to stop laughing during the first run of *The Homecoming* by a member of an audience (it was at the RSC) that looked as if it were composed entirely of British Council pamphlets writers far too busy, I suppose, working out the diagrammatic patterns of the territorial imperative, or making mental jottings of the symbols, myths, paradigms, emblems, to catch the life going on on the stage. This was the first Pinter I'd seen, having been put off his previous stuff by the language of the reviews (the favourable ones, I mean), but my nephew insisted that he'd had a *terrific* time at *The Caretaker*. When I booked the tickets, I told the box office that I was accompanying an elderly relative with a game leg; could we have two on the aisle, please; and reminded my nephew that if by any unlikely chance we stuck it through the first act, we were to treat the interval as the first polite opportunity for returning us to the streets. The highest tribute I can pay the evening is that we spent the interval in the theatre bar, listening quite good-humouredly to the guttural decodings going on all about us.

I suppose, finding myself unexpectedly back at my first Pinter play after all these years, that this is an opportune moment to work in an account of my first meeting with him. It was at his then house in Regent's Park, to which Michael Codron, David Sutton and I had been invited after Michael had sent him the script of *Butley*, with the suggestion that he might like to direct it. We were taken up to his eyrie by, I believe – my memory's not at all clear on this – a housekeeper. Harold was lying on a *chaise-longue* in a black silk shirt (and other garments, like boots and trousers, etc.), a dandy at first glimpse, or something worse even. That was the only time I've seen Harold as if he were posing for *The Yellow Book*, the only time I've seen him stretched on a *chaise-longue*, indeed stretched anywhere.* Normally he stands or sits bolt upright. The only other thing I remember from that first meeting, apart from the incisiveness with which he talked about the play, was his new car, a Mercedes Benz, which had just been delivered, and which fifteen years later he still drives. Michael and David stood on the pavement eyeing it with reverence as he pointed out its body tone, its sultry panelling, its classical this and that. To me, a non-driver, it was a car, if not exactly like any other, not significantly different. In the days when we had a car in the family, I could never remember its make, let alone its licence number. In fact we have owned at various stages three cars. One was small; one was red; the last one was black. That's as far as

* Harold has disputed this version of our meeting – denying that he's ever stretched out full-length in black silk on a *chaise-longue*. I am inclined to believe him, though I am quite unable to understand why my memory has presented me with this image, so uncharacteristic except for the colour of the shirt, as to be virtually a contradiction.

I can go. So Harold's passion for his machine was quite foreign to me. The first subject about which we really began to talk (apart from the play itself) was cricket. I count the intensely companionable summer of 1970 in which we took *Butley* through rehearsals in London, previews in Oxford, and into the West End, as one of the happiest of my life. Harold insisted that I attend all the casting sessions, all the rehearsals, all the previews, and so he released in me the obsessive, which I suspect from time to time he has had reason to regret.

Taken from *An Unnatural Pursuit and Other Pieces* by Simon Gray (Faber and Faber, 1985).

JOHN PILGER

In 1988, the literary critic and novelist D. J. Taylor wrote a seminal piece entitled 'When the Pen Sleeps'. He expanded this into a book, *A Vain Conceit*, in which he wondered why the English novel so often degenerated into 'drawing room twitter' and why the great issues of the day were shunned by writers, unlike their counterparts in, say, Latin America, who felt a *responsibility* to take on politics: the great themes of justice and injustice, wealth and poverty, war and peace. The notion of the writer working in splendid isolation was absurd. Where, he asked, were the George Orwells, the Upton Sinclairs, the John Steinbecks of the modern age?

Twelve years on, Taylor, whose own dissidence as a critic underscored his point, was asking the same question: where was the English Gore Vidal and John Gregory Dunne: 'intellectual heavyweights briskly at large in the political amphitheatre, while we end up with Lord Archer and Douglas Hurd.' The *Guardian*, as I write this, is devoting tombstones of its columns to every tedious, insignificant emission of the king of the drawing room, Martin Amis ('Martin Amis. *The Interview*').

It seems that in the post-modern, celebrity world of writing, prizes are allotted to those who compete for the emperor's threads; the politically unsafe need not apply. John Keane, the chairman of the Orwell Prize for Political Writing, once defended the absence of great contemporary political writers among the Orwell prize-winners not by lamenting the fact and asking why, but by attacking those who referred back to 'an imaginary golden past'. He wrote that those who 'hanker' after this illusory past failed to appreciate writers making sense of 'the collapse of the old left–right divide'.

What collapse? The convergence of the Labour and Tory parties, like the American Democrats with the Republicans, represents a meeting of essentially like minds. Journalists work assiduously to promote a false division between the mainstream parties and to obfuscate the truth that Britain is now a single-ideology state with two competing, almost identical pro-business factions. The real divisions between left and right are to be found outside Parliament and have never been greater. They reflect the unprecedented disparity between the poverty of the majority of humanity and the power and privilege of a corporate and militarist minority, headquartered in Washington, who seek to control the world's resources. One of the reasons these mighty pirates have such a free reign is that the Anglo-American intelligentsia, notably writers, 'the people with voice' as Lord Macaulay called them, are quiet or complicit or craven or twittering, and rich as a result. Thought-provokers pop up from time to time, but the English establishment has always been brilliant at de-fanging and absorbing them. Those who resist assimilation are mocked as eccentrics until they conform to their stereotype and its authorised views.

The unflagging exception is Harold Pinter. The other day, I sat down to compile a list of other writers remotely like him, those 'with a voice' and an understanding of their wider responsibilities as writers. The page was blank save for Pinter. Only he is the unquiet one, the untwitterer, the one with guts, who speaks out. Above all, he understands the problem. Listen to this:

We are in a terrible dip at the moment, a kind of abyss, because the assumption is that politics are all over. That's what the propaganda says. But I don't believe the propaganda. I believe that politics, our political consciousness and our political intelligence are not all over, because if they are, we are really doomed. I can't myself live like this. I've been told so often that I live in a free country, I'm damn well going to be free. By which I mean I'm going to retain my independence of mind and spirit, and I think that's what is obligatory upon all of us. Most political systems talk in such vague language, and it's our responsibility and our duty as citizens of our various countries to exercise acts of critical scrutiny upon that use of language. Of course, that means that one does tend to become rather unpopular. But to hell with that.

I first met Harold when he was supporting the popularly elected government in Nicaragua in the 1980s. I had reported from Nicaragua, and made a film about the remarkable gains of the Sandinistas despite Ronald Reagan's attempts to crush them by illegally sending CIA-trained proxies across the border from Honduras to slit the throats of midwives and other anti-Americans. US foreign policy is unchanged in that respect: the smaller the country the greater the threat. By that, I mean the threat of a good example to other small countries which might seek to alleviate the abject poverty of their people by rejecting American dominance. What struck me about Harold's involvement was his understanding of this truth, which is generally a taboo in the United States and Britain, and the eloquent 'to hell with that' response in everything he said and wrote. (Read his hilarious account of the *Guardian*'s response to his violent poem 'American Football (A Reflection Upon the Gulf War)'.)

Almost single-handedly, it seemed, he restored 'imperialism' to the political lexicon. Remember that no commentator uses this word any more; to utter it in a public place is like shouting 'fuck' in a convent. This was not always the case. Up until the Second World War, the British rulers of much of the world were proud to call themselves imperialists. Unfortunately the unseemly fascists in Germany and Italy also liked to call themselves imperialists, so in the democracies new words had to be deployed, like 'defending freedom against communism'. During the epic American invasion and destruction of Indo-China, which oversaw the deaths of five million people, the maiming and dispossession of millions more and the poisoning of their environment, the word was banned, or used only by opponents. Understandably, now that imperialism has become respectable again, 'humanitarian wars', 'globalisation', etc. are preferred.

Harold Pinter has illuminated these terms as fraudulent, and lies. He has described, correctly, the crushing of Nicaragua, the blockade against Cuba, the wholesale killing of Iraqi and Yugoslav civilians as imperialist atrocities. In illustrating the American crime committed against Nicaragua, and noting that the United States Government had dismissed an International Court of Justice ruling that it stop breaking the law in its murderous attacks, Pinter reminded us that Washington seldom respected international law; and he was right. He wrote:

> In 1965, President Lyndon Johnson said to the Greek Ambassador to the US, 'Fuck your Parliament and your constitution. America is an elephant. Cyprus is a flea. Greece is a flea. If these two fellows keep itching the elephant, they may just get whacked by the elephant's trunk, whacked good . . . '. He meant that. Two years later,

the Colonels took over and the Greek people spent seven years in hell. You have to hand it to Johnson. He sometimes told the truth, however brutal. Reagan tells lies. His celebrated description of Nicaragua as a 'totalitarian dungeon' was a lie from every conceivable angle. It was an assertion unsupported by facts; it had no basis in reality. But it's a good, vivid, resonant phrase which persuaded the unthinking . . .

In his play *Ashes to Ashes*, Pinter uses the images of Nazism and the Holocaust, while interpreting them as a warning against similar 'repressive, cynical and indifferent acts of murder' by the clients of arms-dealing imperialist states such as the United States and Britain. 'The word democracy begins to stink,' he said. 'So in *Ashes to Ashes* I'm not simply talking about the Nazis; I'm talking about us, and our conception of our past and our history, and what it does to us in the present.'

Pinter is not saying the democracies are totalitarian like Nazi Germany, not at all, but that totalitarian actions are taken by impeccably polite democrats and, in principle and effect, are little different from those taken by fascists. The crucial difference is distance from the crime. Half a million people were murdered by American bombers sent secretly and illegally to skies above Cambodia by Nixon and Kissinger, igniting an Asian holocaust, which Pol Pot completed.

The critics have hated Pinter's political work, often attacking his plays mindlessly and patronising his outspokenness. He, in turn, has mocked their empty derision. He is a truth-teller. His speech to, of all people, the Confederation of Analytical Psychologists in 1999, was the most succint analysis of Nato's attack on Yugoslavia I have read. He used facts, not rhetoric, in demolishing the inanities of a 'humanitarian war' and raising the forbidden question of the expanding American oil protectorate in the Caspian Sea region, and the importance of the oil running through Yugoslavia. He quoted the US Energy Secretary, Bill Richardson: 'This is about America's energy security. It's also about preventing strategic inroads by those who don't share our values. We are trying to move these newly independent states (of the former Soviet Union) toward the West. We would like to see them reliant on Western commercial and political interests. We've made a substantial political investment in the Caspian and it's important that both the pipeline map and the politics come out right.'

Pinter's understanding of political language follows Orwell's. He does not, as he would say, give a shit about the propriety of language, only its true sense. At the end of the Cold War in 1989, he wrote, ' . . . for the last forty years, our thought has been trapped in hollow structures of language, a stale, dead but immensely successful rhetoric. This has represented, in my view, a defeat of the intelligence and of the will.'

He never accepted this, of course. Thanks in no small measure to him, defeat is far from assured. On the contrary, while other writers have slept or twittered, he has been aware that people are never still, and indeed are stirring again: the thousands who went to Seattle, the 600,000 who came into the street of Brazilian cities last May Day. Harold Pinter has a place of honour among them, and I salute him.

HILARY WAINWRIGHT

In 1989 we wrote to a large number of well-known left-wing dignitaries asking them for support for a new fortnightly newspaper called *Socialist*. Harold Pinter was one of the few who responded.

He did not know us. We were not friends of friends. We were chatterers but not part of the well-known chattering classes. We simply promised to look at the facts without fear; to inspire confidence in others and ourselves, to imagine, create and work for alternatives.

Harold gave us his support. He also gave us confidence and his example encouraged others. From this I learnt that one of Harold Pinter's distinguishing marks is his courage. His courage to speak out against the powerful. He doesn't wait to find out who else might be supporting a cause. He doesn't wait to find out whether it's fashionable. Harold supports something because he believes in it.

And he really does give support: active and attentive support, with great concern for detail. He doesn't just say, 'OK you've tweaked my conscience; here's the money, now go away and leave me alone.' His conscience drives him; it is not to be placated by offerings to good causes.

When we decided to abandon the fortnightly newspaper and work instead towards founding the monthly magazine, *Red Pepper*, he paid careful attention to all the main decisions to be made: the name, the fund-raising, the first

[49]

issue, the launch. He chaired and directed a historic conversation between Noam Chomsky and John Pilger on the New World Order.

This was at a time when many people were in a state of disorientation brought on by the gloating way in which free market capitalism claimed victory in the Cold War. Amongst many on the left there was a timorous defensive mood. Harold, however, was clear and consistent in his contempt for those in power. His willingness to speak out at a time when Western powers, especially US power, expected deference exposed successive presidents as emperors without clothes.

If only more public intellectuals had Harold's courage to inspire defiance where there is deference, we might achieve a genuine democracy. Thank you, Harold.

ROBERT WINDER

The first time I ran into Harold Pinter was . . . well, when I ran in to him. We were playing cricket in London's Gunnersbury Park. I was the bowler; he was the batsman. I shouldn't have been surprised: we were, after all, playing 'Harold Pinter's XI'. But I had not played against him before, and perhaps naively imagined that his role would be senatorial, if not ceremonial. Yet here he was, striding out to open the batting, taking a gruff guard and eyeing the gaps in the field. I did not know then how characteristic it was that he should be leading from the front, that cricket was not for him some jocular parody of a country house pursuit, that with a bat in his hand he would never stoop to mere messing about.

I was impressed. I'd spent years looking at the photograph of Harold on the back of the Methuen editions of his plays: the strict black roll-neck, that intense inward gaze and modish tilt of the head. It was no small thing to see so revered and famous a profile gently lifting and lowering a bat up there. And it was clear from his stance that he was serious. He looked purposeful. He looked the part.

I was caught in two minds. He was a world-famous play-wright, sure; but what was he like as a batsman? It wouldn't do to ruin his day by getting him out; on the other hand, it couldn't hurt to impress him a bit, if I could. And there was cricketing pride to consider: I didn't want to be smacked around by anyone. In the event I bowled a pretty nice ball. It swung in slightly, and for one panicky, patronising second I was convinced I'd bowled him. I hadn't. Harold leaned forward and drilled it wide of mid-on for four. A few balls later, he did it again. In the years to come (this was 1989) I would learn that Harold was not necessarily a batsman who had, as they say, every shot in the book. But he certainly had this one. Time after time he leaned forward and knocked the ball away on the leg side. The only thing that saved my figures, and my reputation, was the fact that Harold – how to put it? – might have lost an inch or two of pace over years. Experience had taught him how to turn twos into ones. It was less expensive than it might have been.

I can't remember what happened after that. Harold scored twenty or so, I think, then threw it away. I'm pretty sure it wasn't me that got him out. But I must have bowled well enough because afterwards, in a riverside pub, Harold asked me who I usually played for and if I might like to play for him. I said yes (of course) and that was that. In my first brush with Harold's alarming administrative efficiency, I received a fixture list and a cheerful note in the next post.

That was more than ten years ago. Since then I have joined a troupe for whom Harold's voice has become an integral part of the English summer. He's there, like the first cuckoo, on the telephone – 'I've got you down for Wycombe House. Now what about Beddington? It's time we beat those buggers.' His redoubtable affection for cricket runs to the infinite pains he takes over teams and fixtures, long, beady-eyed umpiring stints and the generous standing of rounds in the bar after the game. All the time I've known him, the newspapers have done their damnedest to depict Pinter as a grouchy misanthrope. In truth, it is very hard to buy a drink when Harold is within range. Year after year he subsidises the team's dinner and drinks bills as unobtrusively as if he has no wish even to be thanked.

The game remains, though, at bottom not a social affair, but a contest. To say that Harold loves to win is to miss the point: winning *is* the point. And he gives short shrift to anyone who laughs off defeat too easily. When the team is doing badly, he can be seen nursing his dismay by retiring to his funereal black Mercedes; when we do *really* badly, he drives off in it. But he is a superb applauder: quick to ring or write to congratulate people on a good effort. At a time when the love of cricket is at a low ebb, and too easily lampooned as a sepia-tinted English whimsy – a gentle pastoral idyll of vicars in bicycle clips and I'm-sure-we'd-all-love-to-thank-Barbara-for-her-marvellous-teas – Harold stands for a different tradition, a more urban and exacting idea of cricket as a bold theatre of aggression.

A Londoner, he grew up awed by the Yorkshire and England teams of the 1950s – Hutton and Co. – which best expressed the gritty, heartfelt, uncompromising side of the game. His own club – the Gaieties – might sound raffish, a wandering group of theatrical part-timers; but he has no patience with glad-hats and loves nothing better than to give them a good pasting. He's a Player, not a Gentleman, and his is not a starry team: he wants runs and wickets, not reputations.

There are some larkish moments, though. One year, in that same fixture down in Gunnersbury Park, one of Harold's friends, Salman Rushdie, turned up playing for the opposition. His minders squinted at the ball as if it were a hand grenade. But as luck would have it, the opposing skipper clearly did not know quite how hot a property he had been handed. At one point he turned to a colleague and said:

'That guy down at fine leg. Any idea who he is?'

The man stared in disbelief. 'Yes of course I know who he is,' he said.

There was a pause. 'Well, who is he then?'

Oh my goodness. He really didn't know. 'It's Salman Rushdie, you fool.'

'Oh,' said the skipper, looking hesitant. 'Well . . . can you tell him to go a bit finer?'

These moments are not the norm, however. The sight of Harold's car nosing into the ground makes eleven backs stiffen a bit. At once, the game becomes a serious matter. Harold reserves a special brand of haughty impatience – he is famous for it on many grounds – for people who lose track of the scoreboard or stroll in front of the sightscreen. At other times he can be oblivious to distractions: he is not one of those cricketers who counts the planes buzzing overhead, or notices the kestrel hovering over the railway tracks. I once hoisted a remarkable shot (by my standards) back towards the pavilion: an enormous six. As the ball arched up, everyone on the ground realised it was going to land in a gaggle of small children, and winced. Everyone except Harold, that is. The air was thick with cries of 'Look out!' and 'Jesus Christ!'; and the children screamed and scattered like pigeons. But over and above everything you could hear Harold's grand baritone booming through the hubbub. '*Bloody! Good! Shot!*'

Luckily, the ball hit a flagpole. No one was hurt.

Harold himself enjoys the sometimes incongruous juxtapositions which cricket brings to his life. Once, he threw a pre-match lunch at his house in Notting Hill; some members of the team changed there before heading for the game. Later, Harold had to leave early because Daniel Ortega, President of Nicaragua, was coming for dinner. Harold himself tells the

[54]

story with glee. 'There were these bodyguards, right? . . . And I mean, bloody hell, they were the real thing. Serious. Dark glasses, the whole thing. And the doorbell went, and these bodyguards . . . well, they bloody jumped. And it was the Gaieties, coming to pick up their trousers.'

He loves to recall, too, the time when Joseph Losey was filming *The Go-Between*, and his screenplay required one of the actors to hit a six onto a roof – a risky stage direction which might well have taken hours to accomplish. Harold drafted in a Gaieties colleague, Fred Paolozzi, to attempt the stunt – and he pulled it off at the very first attempt. A first-ball six! Amazing! Losey, however, entirely failed to appreciate the magnificence of the feat, and assumed from the ease with which it had been achieved that it couldn't be that difficult. 'Fine,' he said distractedly. 'OK, let's do it again. Take two.'

Sometimes, this mingling of Harold's worlds is a complete accident. A few years ago I wrote a book about cricket which recounted the following story (forgive me for repeating it here). We were playing Oxted – a nice enough place, though for central Londoners it involved a boring hour or so staggering through the traffic to Surrey. So we weren't too impressed when we arrived to find that the home side had cancelled the game. 'We tried to ring,' they said apologetically. 'But you'd already left.' Harold was furious, and not only on his own behalf – our long-serving West Indian fast bowler had come down that morning on the train from Newcastle, a journey that put our own modest commute into perspective.

Off went an angry letter ('Never in all my years, etc.') to the President, Oxted C.C. Harold sent copies to all of us – except for one man, who opened the package on his doormat to find Harold's recently completed screenplay of *Lolita*.

It was a nice surprise, and the player, a noted novelist in his own right, felt flattered to have been given this sneak preview. He read it at once and, since he lived close by, dropped in on Harold later on, to hand it back and say how much he'd enjoyed it.

'Oh Christ,' said Harold. 'That was supposed to go to Universal.'

It took a moment for the penny to drop. Then the full magic of the mistake sank in. At that very moment, perhaps, Adrian (*Fatal Attraction*) Lyne, the director of *Lolita*, was licking his lips, tearing open his long-awaited new script by Harold Pinter . . . and finding instead a distinctly snotty letter to a cricket club just off the M25.

God knows what he thought. It was certainly a new slant on Nabokov's sprightly masterpiece. Perhaps he felt that it perfectly captured the spirit of the book.

Another time, the Gaieties were playing Roehampton, and Harold's opening batsmen, Ian and Justin, put on 264 without losing a wicket – an unusual partnership in any form of cricket and a club record by far. In honour of the feat I wrote a rum-ti-tum John Betjeman rip-off, which included the following verse:

> Harold commandeers the bar
> (Justin's lager, Ian's wine)
> Recollects his finest hour,
> Caught midwicket, fifty-nine.

Naturally, my description of Harold's finest hour was a guess: I had no idea what his top score was. I had not at that point read his resounding tribute to another Gaieties cricketer, the ex-Somerset and England all-rounder Arthur Wellard, in which Harold recalls Wellard's words of praise after a stoic match-saving innings of twenty-five. 'I was proud of you,' Wellard said. 'I don't suppose any words said to me have given me greater pleasure,' records Harold. So, once again, I was nervous: what if fifty-nine was too low? What kind of an insult would *that* be? Anyway, I sent it off to Harold, thinking it might amuse him, and at once received a sweet and scrupulous reply. He loved it, he said, and would like to send it on to all sorts of people. But there was this one thing . . . his best-ever score was thirty-nine. Would I mind awfully changing it before he sent it out?

Mind? How could I mind (it still rhymed with 'wine', after all)? Thirty-nine it was. And don't you ever forget it.

LINDSAY DUNCAN

———————

Harold had taken Stephen Rea and me for lunch at The Ivy. It was a Saturday in September 1996. We were marking the end of the rehearsal period for *Ashes to Ashes*. The following week the play would be seen by an audience for the first time.

Harold likes to mark things. More recently, at exactly the same point in rehearsals for *The Room* and *Celebration*, I went back into the rehearsal room for something after everybody had gone. Stage management were collecting props and clearing up. Harold was standing looking at the semi-circle of chairs where the company had been ten minutes ago, He turned to me and said tenderly, 'I was just looking and thinking – this is where they all sat . . . '

We had a happy lunch at The Ivy – Stephen had to catch a plane to Dublin so Harold and I were alone with our coffee.

'Now look,' said Harold, 'there's something I'd like to talk to you about. As you know, Roger Michell is going to direct this play of mine at the National. *The Homecoming*. Do you know *The Homecoming*?'

I wondered if I could get away with lying.

'No, no, I'm afraid I don't.'

'Well, it's not a bad play,' said Harold.

Having established that Ruth wasn't a bad part either, I was rather excited, and Harold, on the brink of opening his new play and about to revive another, was pretty excited too.

'I'll get a copy this weekend.'

'I'll have one sent to you.'

'No, it's quicker if I just get one.'

'Quicker' is a good word with Harold.

A few minutes later, work bags in hand, we're marching up the Charing Cross Road on a mission and I'm smiling at how determined we must look for a Saturday afternoon.

There we are in the plays section at Waterstone's looking for 'P' and remarking drily on the poor selection.

'I'll have to have a word with someone,' said Harold.

We find *The Homecoming*. 'I'll get it,' I said.

'No no, allow me.'

'No, please!'

'I insist.'

So Harold handed over the money for a copy of *The Homecoming* to a young man who never raised his eyes from the till.

Harold wrote inside, 'Jesus, I hope you like it!'

I read it on the 24 bus and by the time I got home I was crying I wanted to do it so much.

IAN MCDIARMID *and* JONATHAN KENT

----

*. . . a magnum of champagne. The waiter with a tray of
glasses.*
Matt looks at the label on the bottle.
MATT: That's the best of the best.*

In many ways, the work of Harold Pinter has been the
leitmotif of the Almeida since we became its directors.

Our policy (although we try to avoid that word) is quite
simple – to present the best of the new, in tandem with
revivals of work that might benefit from revaluation – or
even just a fresh look. We are also a theatre where the
relationship between writer, director and actor is paramount.

Harold is, of course, all three.

We have presented seven plays by Harold Pinter in the last
ten years – more than any other playwright – four 'classics',
including the first London revivals of *Betrayal* and *No Man's
Land*, and three world premières, including, in the spring of
this year, his most recent play, aptly if ironically called
Celebration.

Our first meeting was in 1990 when we hoped to persuade
him to agree to a production of *Betrayal* – to head a three-
play season about sexual passion (Wedekind's *Lulu* and
Dryden's *All For Love* were the others).

Initially, he was hesitant. Peter Hall's original National
Theatre production in 1978 – beautifully acted though it was –

had been the victim of industrial disputes and was almost wilfully misunderstood by at least one major critic. We knew it was a masterpiece and the Almeida was the ideal space for it.

Over lunch (and a bottle of champagne), we suggested possible actors – and the choice of David Leveaux as director proved luckily inspired. His forensic attention to detail, coupled with an intense dark lyricism and the ability to make every gesture count make him the ideal Pinter director. Play, acting and production were hailed and Michael Billington did a *volte face*.

Shortly afterwards, Harold telephoned to say he had written *Party Time* and wanted to pair it with a production of *Mountain Language*, brutality and intolerance being the connecting theme. If we liked the idea, he would direct. If we *liked* the idea . . .?

The plays and production, with a crack company, were received with a predictable mix of antagonism and admiration.

So . . . what next?

No Man's Land had not been seen in London for seventeen years, but this mysterious, bleak, very funny play was, up to this point, indelibly associated with two legendary actors giving two of their greatest performances.

'But of course I didn't write it *for* John Gielgud and Ralph Richardson,' Harold announced over another lunch (and another bottle of champagne). He'd had an idea to break the spell of the past.

He'd play Hirst. Perhaps Paul Eddington might play Spooner? And David Leveaux would direct?

It was a moving occasion on many levels, not least to see the writer returning to his roots as an actor, arriving nightly for the 'half', sharing one of the Almeida's two dressing rooms – the other to be used for 'r. and r.' (and, with the prescribed bottle of champagne in the fridge, inevitably christened 'Harry's Bar').

During the run of the play, something else happened, triggered, we like to believe, by the act of acting. Harold literally dreamt a new play. While on holiday in the break between the Almeida run and *No Man's Land*'s transfer to the Comedy Theatre, he wrote his first full-length work since *Betrayal*. *Moonlight* heralded Ian Holm's return to the stage after a long absence, and the definitive 'Lenny' in *The Homecoming* was – like the writer – once again revealed at the height of his powers.

Towards the end of last year, just as we were thinking of how the Almeida might contribute to the celebration of his seventieth birthday, his agent, Judy Daish, telephoned. Harold had written a new play called *Celebration*. Would we be interested in doing it?

It arrived half an hour before an opening night. We read it after the performance and scheduled it the following morning (and sent him a bottle of champagne).

Under the author's immaculate direction and partnered by his first, but rarely seen, play *The Room*, this mordant, wildly funny, passionate and brilliantly acted piece ushered us into the new millennium and another decade of Harold Pinter's astonishing creativity.

LAMBERT: Plenty of celebrations to come. Rest assured.
MATT: Plenty to celebrate.*

Cheers, Harold.

* The quotations are from *Celebration* by Harold Pinter.

PEGGY PATERSON

'Come on, we're having lunch with Harold and we cannot, under any circumstances, be late,' Robert McCrum, Faber's editorial director, said to me on my first week as Drama Editor. 'Nervous?' enquired Robert. 'No,' I lied.

It was October 1994. With a list of playwrights made up of the best writers around, being Drama Editor at Faber and Faber was a dream job. There they were, established, in all their glowing greatness. And there I was, an unknown quantity, hoping to 'do' things. It was impossible not to be in awe. Especially of Harold Pinter: the breadth and depth of his talent displayed in a shelf full of books in my new office, and his unwavering commitment to his beliefs, written about over the years in newspapers and magazines. However, admiration from afar wasn't quite the same as sitting across the table from him in a smart restaurant in Holland Park, attempting to articulate my plans for his published work, plans for the Drama list as a whole – and eat and drink at the same time.

So, in awe, yes, expecting penetrating questions, yes, and unfeasibly worried that my lack of specific political knowledge might make me look a complete idiot. (A friend of mine is married to a Kurdish man so, as part of my preparation, I went round and talked to him for two hours about 'the situation'.) I can't now imagine why I might have thought that Harold Pinter would want to wrong-foot me. But what

I really was not prepared for was the warmth and generosity of the man. He put me at my ease, he listened and commented favourably. He was and is genuinely interested in all parts of publication, from design to production. But he was especially keen to talk about young writers and their writing. His encouragement to other writers is recorded elsewhere in this collections of essays, but it was so enjoyable to be able to talk about plans for bringing new writers onto the list and to be met with enthusiastic responses from Harold.

Since then, there have been many more meetings. Working together on *Various Voices*, his collection of prose, poetry and political writings from 1948 to 1998, was an especial treat. Reading a lot of material, much of it previously unpublished, really did build up a picture of a writer of stature and a man of integrity. And there was no pussyfooting around when it came to cutting material, or cutting pieces altogether: 'Peggy, I've thought about it and that goes, and that goes, and that goes. Okay.' Not so much a question, more of an assertion. However, I did argue for the inclusion of one or two pieces destined for the chop.

'Everybody's seen that one before.'

'Yes, but it's a particular favourite of mine.'

'Is it? Okay, let's keep it.'

Harold does not waste words but his appreciation of work done by others is unstinting and unfailingly generous.

There's no getting away from it, meeting Harold is still an event, even after several years. You'd better have your wits, and your facts, about you. And if you're going to argue, then marshall your thoughts first. But then you can really enjoy the conversation with one of the most talented writers of the twentieth and twenty-first centuries.

Henry Woolf

The old bull surges on,

Various hyenas clinging to its flanks.

'What is it with him?'

'Someone's always been kicking the shit out of someone.'

'That's history.'

'It's not as if we're unaware.'

'He could be beautiful.'

'Beautiful.'

'But no, he has to stir it up, stir it up.'

'Kurds? What the fuck are Kurds?'

BIOGRAPHICAL NOTES

ALAN BATES made his West End début in 1956. His theatre work ranges from his creation of the role of Cliff in John Osborne's *Look Back in Anger* to Dennis Potter's adaptation of *The Mayor of Casterbridge* for the BBC. In betweeen, he has starred in many acclaimed productions in London, Stratford, Los Angeles and New York, including Harold Pinter's *The Caretaker*. In addition to his many television performances he has acted in more than fifty films and received an Academy Award nomination for *The Fixer*.

EILEEN DISS has worked as a freelance designer for theatre, film and television since 1959. Among her many productions, she has worked on Harold Pinter's *The Caretaker*, *The Homecoming*, *The Hothouse*, *Ashes to Ashes*, *Betrayal*, *The Room* and *Celebration*, and *The Tea Party* (television). She has received four BAFTA Television Design Awards.

LINDSAY DUNCAN appeared in Harold Pinter's *The Room* and *Celebration* (Almeida), *The Homecoming* (NT) and *Ashes to Ashes* (Royal Court). She was awarded an Olivier for *Les Liaisons Dangereuses* and Evening Standard Best Actress for *Cat on a Hot Tin Roof*. Her appearances for television include *Oliver Twist*, *Shooting the Past*, *The Rector's Wife* (Nymphe d'Argent award), *GBH* and *Traffik*, and for film, *Mansfield Park*, *An Ideal Husband*, *City Hall* and *The Reflecting Sun*.

RICHARD EYRE, former director of the Royal National Theatre, has directed numerous classics, including *King Lear* with Ian Holm (also for BBC TV) and world premières of plays by Tom Stoppard, Alan Bennett, Trevor Griffiths, Christopher Hampton and David Hare – most recently *Amy's View* on Broadway. His films for television include *Tumbledown*, *The Insurance Man* and *The Ploughman's Lunch*. His autobiography, *Utopia and Other Places*, is published by Bloomsbury.

SIMON GRAY. Pinter has directed eight of his plays (*Butley*, *Otherwise Engaged*, *The Rear Column*, *Close of Play*, *Quartermaine's Terms*, *The Common Pursuit*, *Life Support* and *The Late Middle Classes*), one film (*Butley*) and one television film (*The Rear Column*).

DAVID HARE was born in Sussex in 1947. In 1970 his first play *Slag* was performed at the Hampstead Theatre Club. In 1993 three of his plays, *Racing Demon*, *Murmuring Judges* and *The Absence of War*, were presented together in repertory at the Olivier Theatre in London. Since 1983, nine of his best-known plays, including *Plenty*, *The Secret Rapture*, *Skylight*, *The Judas Kiss*, *Amy's View* and *Via Dolorosa* have also been presented on Broadway.

RONALD HARWOOD's plays include *The Dresser*, *Another Time*, *Taking Sides* and *Quartet*. He is also the author of *Sir Donald Wolfit, CBE: His Life and Work in the Unfashionable Theatre*, and a history of the theatre, *All the World's a Stage*. He is the editor of *The Faber Book of the Theatre*.

DOUGLAS HODGE has worked with Harold Pinter on *Moonlight* and *No Man's Land* in the West End, *The Lover* and *The Collection* at the Donmar Warehouse, *Betrayal* at the RNT and *The Proust Screenplay* on BBC Radio. Other RNT productions include *Pericles*, *King Lear* and *Blinded by the Sun*. He has appeared in many BBC, Thames, Granada and Channel Four TV productions, and his film work includes *The Trial*, *Bliss* and *Saigon Baby*.

PATRICK MARBER was born in London in 1956. He is the author of *Dealer's Choice*, *After Miss Julie* and *Closer*. His production of *The Caretaker* will open at the Comedy Theatre in November 2000.

LOUIS MARKS has been a scriptwriter since 1958. A founding editor of *Books and Bookmen*, he joined the BBC in 1970 as Script Editor, moving on to Producer (Film and TV Drama) in 1976. His productions include *The Lost Boys*, *Loving*, *Memento Mori*, *The Trial* and the award-winning 1994 TV adaptation of *Middlemarch*.

IAN McDIARMID and JONATHAN KENT have been joint Artistic Directors of the Almeida Theatre since 1990, where Ian McDiarmid has acted in a number of leading roles, including *Volpone*, Arnolphe in *The School for Wives*, *The Jew of Malta*, and Prospero in *The Tempest*. Productions he has directed include *Scenes from an Execution*, *The Rehearsal* (also West End), and the opera *Siren Song*. Jonathan Kent has directed for the Almeida *When We Dead Waken*, Dryden's *All for Love*, *Medea* (also West End and Broadway), *Chatsky*, *The Showman*, *The School for Wives*, *Gangster No. 1*, *Tartuffe*, *The Life of Galileo*, *The Rules of the Game*, *Ivanov*, *The Government Inspector*, *Hamlet* (also Broadway), Pirandello's *Naked* (also West End), Racine's *Phèdre* and *Britannicus* (also New York), *Plenty*, and *Richard II* and *Coriolanus* (also New York).

EDNA O'BRIEN'S most recent works are a biography of James Joyce, *Wild December*, and a play, *Our Father*, produced at the Almeida Theatre, 1999.

PEGGY PATERSON has been the Drama Editor at Faber and Faber since October 1994.

JOHN PILGER was born and educated in Sydney, Australia. He has been a war correspondent, film-maker and best-selling author. Based in London, he has written from many countries and has twice won British journalism's highest award, that of Journalist of the Year, for his work in Vietnam and Cambodia. Among a number of other awards, he has been International Reporter of the Year. His documentaries have won Academy Awards in Britain and the United States.

HILARY WAINWRIGHT is Editor of *Red Pepper*, the monthly magazine of the independent left. She is a Research Fellow at the Centre for International Labour Studies, Manchester University. Her books include *Beyond the Fragments* (with Lynne Segal and Sheila Rowbotham) and *Labour: a Tale of Two Parties* and *Arguments for a New Left: Answering the Free-Market Right*. She is currently working on a new book, *Reinventing People's Democracy*.

JANET WHITAKER grew up in Leeds and graduated from Manchester University with a degree in Drama. After helping to found Interplay Community Arts, she worked as a teacher, then joined the BBC as a producer in 1977 – first in Education then in the Drama Department in Radio. She has directed Dirk Bogarde, Kathleen Turner and now Harold Pinter, and thinks it is the best job in the world.

PENELOPE WILTON was born in 1947. In her thirty-odd years of acting she has worked for every major theatre company in England in roles both classical and modern, including Karel Reisz's award-winning production of Terence Rattigan's *The Deep Blue Sea* and Harold Pinter's *Betrayal, Moonlight* and A *Kind of Alaska*, for which she won an Irish Theatre Award for Best Actress. Her extensive television and film work includes *Cry Freedom, The French Lieutenant's Woman* and, for the BBC, Pinter's production of *Landscape*.

ROBERT WINDER was formerly Literary Editor of the *Independent* and Deputy Editor of *Granta* magazine. He has written two novels, and is also the author of *Hell for Leather*, a book about modern cricket.

HENRY WOOLF, who lives in Saskatoon, Canada, is Artistic Director of Shakespeare on the Saskatchewan. He is the director of the original production of Harold Pinter's first play *The Room*, and has also acted and directed in London, Paris and New York. He retired in 1997 as Head of the University of Saskatchewan Drama Department.

Works by Harold Pinter

ASHES TO ASHES

BETRAYAL

THE BIRTHDAY PARTY

THE CARETAKER

CELEBRATION and THE ROOM

THE COLLECTION and THE LOVER

THE HOMECOMING

LANDSCAPE and SILENCE

NO MAN'S LAND

OLD TIMES

ONE FOR THE ROAD

OTHER PLACES
(A Kind of Alaska, Victoria Station, Family Voices)

THE ROOM and THE DUMB WAITER

A SLIGHT ACHE and other plays

TEA PARTY and other plays

MOUNTAIN LANGUAGE

PARTY TIME

MOONLIGHT

PLAYS ONE
(The Birthday Party, The Room, The Dumb Waiter,
A Slight Ache, The Hothouse, A Night Out,
The Black and White, The Examination)